Cloud Security and Management:

The Primer on Enterprise Cybersecurity Strategy (Fast Forward Your Security Career)

SIRANJEEVI DHEENADHAYALAN

Product Manager, Security Products at Hashicorp

There are only two types of organizations: Those that have been hacked and those that don't know it yet!

John T. Chambers

Table of Contents

Chapter 1: Introduction to Cybersecurity

The importance of cybersecurity cannot be overstated in the interconnected world of today, where data flows freely and technology is deeply integrated into every aspect of our lives. Hackers, cybercriminals, and even state-sponsored actors are constantly trying to exploit vulnerabilities for personal gain, making cyber threats a significant issue. Awareness and a comprehensive understanding of cybersecurity principles, and strategies are required to safeguard themselves, their organizations, and society as a whole from cyber threats.

Consider the scenario of online shopping. When you enter your credit card details to purchase something, you trust that your information will remain secure. Cybersecurity ensures that your data is encrypted and protected from hackers who might attempt to steal it. Without robust cybersecurity measures, your financial information could be compromised, leading to identity theft or financial loss.

Email, messaging apps, and social media platforms are integral to modern communication. Cybersecurity ensures that our conversations remain private and secure. For example, end-to-end encryption in messaging apps like Signal or WhatsApp ensures that only the sender and receiver can read the messages, protecting them from interception by third parties.

Governments around the world rely on cybersecurity to protect sensitive information and critical infrastructure. For example, cybersecurity defenses are essential for safeguarding military networks from cyber espionage or sabotage attempts by foreign actors. Additionally, cybersecurity plays a crucial role in defending against cyberattacks on national utilities, financial systems, and government agencies.

The proliferation of internet-connected devices, from smart thermostats to wearable fitness trackers, has created new challenges for cybersecurity. These devices collect vast amounts of personal data, raising concerns about privacy and security. For instance, a hacker gaining access to a smart home's security cameras could invade the occupants' privacy. Effective cybersecurity measures are necessary to protect IoT devices and the sensitive data they collect.

So, cybersecurity is not just a concern for IT professionals or cybersecurity experts—it's a fundamental aspect of our daily lives. Whether we're shopping online, communicating with friends and family, running a business, or even safeguarding national security, understanding cybersecurity is essential for protecting ourselves and our digital assets. By staying informed about cybersecurity best practices and adopting proactive measures, we can all contribute to a safer and more secure digital environment.

The Fascinating Evolution of Cyber Threats

As technology advances, so do the tactics of cybercriminals. The evolution of cyber threats is a captivating journey marked by innovation, adaptation, and constant change. Let's delve into the fascinating history of cyber threats, from the early days of computer viruses to the sophisticated techniques used by hackers today.

The story of cyber threats begins with the creation of the first computer virus, the "Creeper" virus, in the early 1970s. This primitive malware spread through ARPANET, displaying a message that read, "I'm the creeper, catch me if you can!" Since then, cybercriminals have developed countless variations of viruses, worms, and Trojans to infect and compromise computer systems.

In the 1990s and early 2000s, malware became increasingly prevalent with the rise of the internet. Examples include the Melissa virus, which spread through infected email attachments, and the Conficker worm, which exploited vulnerabilities in Windows operating systems. Malware evolved to become more sophisticated, employing techniques such as polymorphism and encryption to evade detection by antivirus software.

Cybercriminals realized that exploiting human psychology could be just as effective as exploiting technical vulnerabilities. Phishing attacks, for example, deceive users into divulging sensitive

4

information by masquerading as legitimate entities. An infamous example is the 2016 phishing attack on John Podesta, chairman of Hillary Clinton's presidential campaign, which resulted in the leak of thousands of sensitive emails.

Ransomware emerged as a lucrative form of cybercrime, with attackers encrypting victims' data and demanding payment in exchange for decryption keys. Notable examples include the WannaCry and NotPetya attacks, which caused widespread disruption and financial loss. Ransomware-as-a-Service (RaaS) platforms have further democratized this form of cybercrime, allowing even novice hackers to launch attacks for profit.

State-sponsored cyberattacks, known as advanced persistent threats (APTs), represent a new frontier in cyber warfare. These attacks are characterized by stealth, sophistication, and long-term persistence. For example, the Stuxnet worm, believed to be developed by the United States and Israel, targeted Iran's nuclear facilities with unprecedented precision, sabotaging centrifuges used for uranium enrichment.

The dark web has become a haven for cybercriminals, providing a platform for buying and selling illicit goods and services. Cybercrime marketplaces offer everything from stolen credit card information to zero-day exploits, enabling hackers to launch sophisticated attacks with minimal effort. Law enforcement agencies face significant challenges in combating cybercrime on the dark web due to its anonymity and encryption.

The evolution of cyber threats is a testament to the ingenuity and adaptability of cybercriminals. From the humble beginnings of computer viruses to the sophisticated techniques used in modern cyber attacks, the landscape of cybersecurity is in a constant state of flux.

Intricacies Behind Digital Intrusion

Understanding the anatomy of a cyber attack is crucial for developing effective defense strategies and mitigating the risk of digital intrusion. But what exactly goes on behind the scenes of a cyber attack? Let's unravel the intricate anatomy of a cyber attack, exploring its various stages and methodologies with relatable examples.

Reconnaissance Phase - Gathering Intel:
Every successful cyber attack begins with reconnaissance. Hackers scour the internet for vulnerabilities, using tools like port scanners and social engineering techniques to gather information. For instance, imagine a hacker researching a company on social media to identify key employees and potential entry points into their network.

Initial Access - Breaking In :
Once a target is identified, the next step is gaining initial access. This can be achieved through various means, such as exploiting software vulnerabilities or tricking users into clicking on malicious links. Consider the scenario of a phishing email disguised as a legitimate message from a bank, prompting recipients to enter their login credentials on a fake website.

Privilege Escalation: Obtaining Higher-Level Access:
After gaining initial access, hackers seek to escalate their privileges within the target network. They exploit vulnerabilities in system configurations or leverage stolen credentials to gain higher-level access rights.

For example, a hacker who initially gained access to a user account might exploit a privilege escalation vulnerability to gain administrative privileges.

Lateral Movement: Spreading Across the Network:

With elevated privileges, hackers move laterally across the network, exploring and compromising additional systems and resources. They deploy tools like remote access Trojans (RATs) or exploit weak network segmentation to navigate through the network undetected. Think of a hacker maneuvering through a corporate network, hopping from one compromised machine to another like a digital intruder.

Data Exfiltration: Stealing Sensitive Information:

The ultimate goal of many cyber attacks is to steal valuable data for financial gain or espionage purposes. Hackers exfiltrate sensitive information by copying it to external servers or cloud storage, often using encryption to evade detection. Consider a cybercriminal extracting customer credit card details from a compromised e-commerce website, ready to be sold on the dark web.

Covering Tracks: Erasing Digital Footprints:

To avoid detection and maintain access for future attacks, hackers cover their tracks by deleting log files, altering timestamps, or installing backdoors for continued access. They aim to leave behind minimal evidence of their intrusion, making it challenging for security analysts to identify and mitigate the attack. Imagine a burglar wiping away fingerprints and erasing security camera footage after a break-in.

Price Tag of Cybercrime

Beyond the headlines and the technical jargon lies a very real and tangible cost – one that extends far beyond the virtual realm and directly impacts individuals, businesses, and society at large.

The most obvious impact of cybercrime is financial. Businesses of all sizes are targeted by cybercriminals aiming to steal sensitive information or extort money through ransomware attacks. For example, in 2019, the city of Baltimore fell victim to a ransomware attack that cost an estimated $18.2 million in damages and recovery efforts. Similarly, Equifax, one of the largest credit reporting agencies, suffered a data breach in 2017 that exposed the personal information of over 147 million people, resulting in settlements and fines amounting to hundreds of millions of dollars.

Beyond the immediate financial losses, cyberattacks can inflict severe damage to a company's reputation. The fallout from a data breach can erode customer trust and loyalty, leading to long-term consequences for a brand's bottom line. Take the case of Target, which suffered a massive data breach in 2013. The incident not only cost the company over $200 million but also tarnished its reputation, resulting in a significant drop in sales and ongoing legal battles.

Cybercriminals often target businesses to steal valuable intellectual property, including trade secrets, proprietary algorithms, and research data. This theft can have far-reaching implications, affecting innovation and competitiveness within industries. For example, the Chinese military's alleged hacking of American companies for trade secrets has been a longstanding concern, with estimates suggesting billions of dollars in losses annually for U.S. businesses.

The cost of cybercrime isn't limited to financial and corporate realms; it also takes a personal toll on individuals. Identity theft, online scams, and cyberbullying are just a few examples of how cybercrime directly impacts people's lives. Victims can suffer emotional distress, financial hardship, and even physical harm as a result of malicious online activities.

Beyond the individual and corporate level, cybercrime also poses broader societal challenges. From disrupting critical infrastructure to spreading disinformation and undermining democratic processes, cyberattacks can have profound consequences for the stability and security of entire nations. The 2017 NotPetya attack, for instance, targeted Ukrainian infrastructure but caused collateral damage on a global scale, affecting businesses and organizations worldwide.

The cost of cybercrime extends far beyond the financial losses reported in corporate balance sheets. It affects individuals, businesses, and society as a whole, eroding trust, stifling innovation, and posing significant challenges to security and stability.

Chapter 2: Fundamentals of Cybersecurity

Exploring the CIA Triad in Everyday Life

In the digital age, where information flows freely and swiftly, ensuring the protection of sensitive data is paramount. Enter the CIA Triad: Confidentiality, Integrity, and Availability. The CIA Triad serves as a guiding principle in navigating the complexities of information security, reminding us of the importance of confidentiality, integrity, and availability in safeguarding our digital assets. Let's delve deeper into each aspect with relatable examples from our daily lives.

Confidentiality:
Imagine you're entrusted with a friend's deepest secret. Upholding confidentiality means safeguarding this information from unauthorized access. Just as you wouldn't share your friend's secret without their consent, organizations employ encryption, access controls, and secure communication channels to ensure sensitive data remains private. For instance, healthcare providers protect patient records to maintain confidentiality, respecting their privacy and complying with legal regulations like HIPAA (Health Insurance Portability and Accountability Act).

Integrity:
Integrity ensures that data remains accurate, trustworthy, and unaltered. Consider the game of Chinese whispers, where a message gets distorted

as it passes from one person to another. Similarly, data can be corrupted or manipulated without proper safeguards. Financial institutions employ checksums and digital signatures to verify the authenticity of transactions, preventing tampering or fraudulent activities. In essence, maintaining data integrity ensures that information retains its intended meaning and reliability, fostering trust among users.

Availability:
Availability emphasizes timely and reliable access to information when needed. Picture a library where books are readily accessible to patrons. Likewise, digital services strive to minimize downtime and ensure uninterrupted access for users. Cloud computing platforms employ redundancy and failover mechanisms to mitigate service disruptions, guaranteeing high availability even in the face of hardware failures or cyber attacks. Whether it's accessing emails, streaming content, or conducting online transactions, users rely on the availability of services for seamless digital experiences.

The Art of Risk Management

Effective risk management is no longer a luxury but a necessity. By embracing the principles of cybersecurity risk management and adopting a proactive approach to defense, organizations and individuals alike can navigate the digital frontier with confidence. The National Institute of Standards and Technology (NIST) released the Cybersecurity Framework in 2014, emphasizing risk management and providing a flexible framework for organizations to assess and improve their cybersecurity posture.

One of the first steps in developing cybersecurity policies is conducting a comprehensive risk assessment. Organizations must identify their vulnerabilities and assess the potential impact of cyber threats on their operations. This process involves evaluating the sensitivity of data, the likelihood of various threats, and the effectiveness of existing security measures.

Knowledge is power in the world of cybersecurity. By staying informed about emerging threats and attack vectors, organizations can better prepare themselves to defend against potential breaches. Leveraging threat intelligence feeds and collaborating with industry peers can provide valuable insights into the tactics and techniques employed by cyber adversaries.

No system is immune to vulnerabilities, but proactive management can help minimize the risk. This involves regularly scanning networks and applications for weaknesses, patching known vulnerabilities, and implementing robust security controls to mitigate potential risks.

Despite best efforts, breaches may still occur. A robust incident response plan is essential for minimizing the impact of cyber attacks and restoring normal operations swiftly. This includes clear protocols for detecting, containing, and remediating security incidents, as well as communication strategies for keeping stakeholders informed.

Building Robust Cybersecurity Policies and Procedures

Based on the findings of the risk assessment, an organization must develop clear and concise cybersecurity policies that outline acceptable behaviors and practices for employees and stakeholders. These policies should cover areas such as data protection, access control, incident response, and employee training.

The security operations team in an organization must translate policies into actionable procedures that detail step-by-step guidelines for employees to follow in various scenarios. This includes procedures for securely handling data, reporting security incidents, and responding to cyber threats.

Human error remains one of the leading causes of security breaches, making employee education and training a critical component of cybersecurity efforts. Provide ongoing training sessions and awareness programs to educate employees about cybersecurity best practices, phishing scams, and the importance of following established policies and procedures.

In addition to this, an organization must schedule regular reviews of policies and procedures to ensure they remain effective and up-to-date with the latest security standards and regulatory requirements. This should be initiated at the CISO (Chief Information Security Officer) or at a company's leadership level to safeguard their sensitive information, intellectual property and others.

Developing and implementing cybersecurity policies and procedures is an ongoing process that requires proactive planning, collaboration, and continuous improvement. By conducting risk assessments, establishing clear policies, implementing procedural controls, educating employees, and regularly reviewing and updating policies, organizations can enhance their cyber resilience and protect against evolving threats in today's digital landscape.

Chapter 3: Cybersecurity Technologies and Tools

Security operations professionals play a crucial role in safeguarding their organizations against these evolving threats. A sophisticated security operations personnel must leverage threat intelligence to proactively identify and mitigate potential risks. By integrating threat intelligence feeds into their security infrastructure, organizations can stay informed about emerging threats and anticipate attackers' tactics. For instance, utilizing platforms like Recorded Future or ThreatConnect enables analysts to correlate threat indicators with internal security data, providing actionable insights into potential vulnerabilities and attack vectors.

Automation and orchestration tools streamline security operations by automating repetitive tasks and orchestrating responses to security incidents. For example, Security Orchestration, Automation, and Response (SOAR) platforms like Splunk Phantom or Demisto enable organizations to automate incident response workflows, reducing response times and minimizing manual errors. By automating routine tasks such as threat hunting, malware analysis, and incident triage, security operations teams can focus their efforts on more strategic initiatives.

Traditional perimeter-based security models are no longer sufficient to protect modern enterprise networks. Zero Trust Architecture (ZTA) assumes that threats can originate from both inside and outside the network, requiring strict access controls and continuous verification of user identities.

Implementing Zero Trust principles helps organizations minimize the risk of unauthorized access and lateral movement by segmenting network resources and enforcing least privilege access policies. Real-world examples of Zero Trust implementations include Google's BeyondCorp framework and Microsoft's Zero Trust strategy, which prioritize identity and device authentication to secure access to corporate resources regardless of network location.

As enterprises embrace cloud computing, securing cloud environments becomes paramount for maintaining data confidentiality and regulatory compliance. CSPM solutions like Palo Alto Networks Prisma Cloud and AWS Security Hub help organizations assess their cloud security posture, identify misconfigurations, and enforce compliance with industry regulations. By continuously monitoring cloud infrastructure for security risks and compliance violations, CSPM solutions enable security operations teams to proactively address potential threats and vulnerabilities before they impact business operations.

Firewalls and Intrusion Detection Systems

Firewalls serve as the first line of defense, regulating traffic between internal networks and external entities, such as the internet. They operate by enforcing predetermined security policies, filtering incoming and outgoing traffic based on parameters like IP addresses, ports, and protocols. For instance, a next-generation firewall (NGFW) might utilize deep packet inspection to analyze packet contents and identify malicious payloads. Consider a multinational corporation with offices worldwide. By deploying a centralized firewall solution with unified threat management (UTM) capabilities, the organization can efficiently manage and enforce consistent security policies across its diverse network infrastructure. This approach ensures uniform protection against external threats while facilitating secure communication among geographically dispersed teams.

IDS complement firewalls by providing real-time monitoring and analysis of network traffic to detect suspicious activities or potential security breaches. They utilize signature-based detection, anomaly detection, or behavioral analysis techniques to identify deviations from normal behavior, alerting security teams to potential threats promptly. Imagine an e-commerce platform experiencing a surge in traffic during a flash sale event. Amidst the increased activity, an IDS detects a series of anomalous login attempts originating from multiple geolocations within a short timeframe. Recognizing this as a potential distributed denial-of-service (DDoS) attack, the IDS triggers alerts, enabling security personnel to promptly mitigate the threat by implementing rate-limiting measures and blocking suspicious IP addresses.

Antivirus and Anti-malware Solutions

Antivirus and antimalware solutions play a pivotal role in defending against these threats by detecting, blocking, and removing malicious software from endpoints and networks. Modern antivirus solutions employ a variety of techniques, including signature-based detection, heuristic analysis, and machine learning algorithms, to identify and neutralize threats in real-time. For instance, tools like Symantec Endpoint Protection and McAfee Endpoint Security utilize advanced threat intelligence and behavioral analysis to proactively thwart malware infections. Implementing antivirus and antimalware solutions effectively requires a strategic approach. Security operations professionals should start by conducting a thorough risk assessment to identify potential vulnerabilities and prioritize protection measures accordingly. Additionally, regular software updates and patches are crucial to ensuring that antivirus solutions remain effective against emerging threats. For instance, the widespread adoption of cloud-based antivirus solutions, such as Microsoft Defender Antivirus, offers enterprises real-time threat protection and centralized management capabilities. Modern antivirus and antimalware solutions leverage advanced behavioral analysis techniques to identify previously unknown threats based on their suspicious activities. Consider a situation where a zero-day exploit targets a vulnerability in a widely used software application within an enterprise environment. Traditional signature-based detection methods may fail to recognize the newly emerged threat. However, with behavioral analysis capabilities, security operations professionals can detect anomalous behavior indicative of a potential attack, allowing them to take preemptive action before the threat escalates.

Encryption

At its core, encryption is the process of converting plaintext data into ciphertext, rendering it unintelligible to unauthorized parties. This transformation occurs through complex algorithms and cryptographic keys, ensuring that only authorized entities possess the means to decrypt and access the original information. Think of encryption as a digital vault, safeguarding your data from prying eyes as it traverses networks and storage systems.

To demystify encryption, let's delve into a real-world analogy. Imagine you have a top-secret message that you want to transmit securely to a colleague. You encase this message in a sturdy lockbox, known as encryption, and hand over the key to your colleague. Only they possess the corresponding key to unlock the box and reveal the message within. In the digital realm, encryption employs algorithms like AES (Advanced Encryption Standard) or RSA (Rivest-Shamir-Adleman), coupled with cryptographic keys, to perform this intricate process.

Consider a payment processor transmitting sensitive customer information, such as credit card details, over the internet. By employing encryption protocols such as SSL/TLS, the data is encrypted before transmission, ensuring that even if intercepted by malicious actors, it remains incomprehensible without the corresponding decryption key. This robust encryption mechanism shields the data from eavesdropping and interception, preserving the confidentiality and integrity of customer information. In ontorprioc cnvironments, data-at-rest encryption plays a pivotal role in protecting stored information from unauthorized access. Solutions like BitLocker for Windows and FileVault for macOS encrypt entire disk volumes, thwarting data breaches even if physical storage devices fall into the wrong hands. Hashing represents another crucial aspect of data security, offering a mechanism for data integrity verification and authentication. Unlike encryption, which aims to conceal data, hashing generates a fixed-size alphanumeric string, known as a hash value, from input data. This irreversible process ensures that even minor alterations to the input data produce drastically different hash values, making it ideal for detecting tampering and ensuring data integrity.

Imagine an enterprise storing user passwords in a database. Instead of storing plaintext passwords, the system hashes each password using a cryptographic hash function such as SHA-256. When a user attempts to log in, the system hashes the entered password and compares it to the stored hash value. If the two hashes match, access is granted. This hashing mechanism protects user passwords from being compromised, as even if the database is breached, the hashed passwords remain unintelligible to attackers.

Hash-based Message Authentication Code (HMAC) can add another layer of authentication. This mechanism combines hashing with a secret key to generate a unique authentication tag for data integrity and authentication. By appending this authentication tag to the hashed data, HMAC ensures that both the integrity and the authenticity of the message are preserved, protecting against tampering and unauthorized access.

By understanding the fundamentals of encryption, hashing, and HMAC, security operations professionals can fortify their digital fortresses against the relentless onslaught of cyber threats, ensuring the confidentiality, integrity, and authenticity of their enterprise's most valuable assets. So, arm yourselves with knowledge, stay vigilant, and continue to defend your organization against the forces of digital darkness.

Multi-factor Authentication (MFA) and Passkeys

Multi-factor authentication (MFA) is a security measure that requires users to provide two or more forms of verification before granting access to a system or application. These factors typically include something the user knows (like a password), something they have (such as a security token or passkey), or something they are (like biometric data). Consider a scenario where an employee attempts to log into the company's network remotely. With MFA enabled, the employee not only needs to enter their username and password but also verify their identity using a unique passkey generated by an authenticator app on their smartphone. This additional layer of security significantly reduces the risk of unauthorized access, even if the username and password are compromised. Okta, Duo Secuirty, Google Authenticator, Microsoft authenticator are popular multi-factor authentication applications in the market.

Passkeys, also known as security keys or tokens, are physical or digital devices used to authenticate a user's identity. Unlike traditional passwords that are susceptible to phishing attacks and brute-force hacking attempts, passkeys generate unique codes or signals that are difficult to replicate without physical possession of the key.

Imagine an IT administrator accessing critical systems within the enterprise infrastructure. By utilizing a hardware security key, the administrator adds an extra layer of protection beyond traditional username/password authentication. Even if an attacker manages to obtain the administrator's credentials, they would still require physical access to the security key to gain entry, greatly mitigating the risk of unauthorized access.

Secure Software Development Lifecycle (SDLC)

The SDLC encompasses the entire process of software development, from inception to deployment and maintenance. It comprises several phases, including planning, design, implementation, testing, deployment, and maintenance. Each stage presents unique security challenges, necessitating a comprehensive security strategy woven into the fabric of the development process.

Consider the notorious case of Equifax, where a vulnerability in Apache Struts went unnoticed, leading to a massive data breach affecting millions of individuals. This incident underscores the criticality of integrating security seamlessly into the SDLC. Similarly, the heartbleed bug, discovered in the OpenSSL cryptographic software library in 2014, highlighted the importance of thorough testing in the SDLC. This critical vulnerability allowed attackers to exploit a flaw in the implementation of the Transport Layer Security (TLS) protocol, potentially exposing sensitive data transmitted over secure connections.

During the planning phase, security teams collaborate with developers to identify potential areas of vulnerability and establish security requirements. This involves defining policies for handling secrets, implementing access controls, and integrating secret managers and scanning tools into the development pipeline.

During the testing and deployment phase, CI/CD (Continuous integration/ Continuous delivery) is the practice of frequently integrating code changes into a shared repository, followed by automated builds and tests. Security operations professionals can enhance CI/CD processes by integrating static security checks with tools like SonarQube or Gitguardian and dynamic application security testing (DAST) to identify vulnerabilities.

Secrets, such as API keys and credentials, are often embedded within code repositories, posing significant security risks if exposed. Security operations professionals must implement secrets scanning tools to automatically identify and remove hardcoded secrets. Popular secret scanning solutions in the market includes Trufflehog, gitguardian, spectralOps, Github Advanced Security, Vault Radar etc..

Chapter 4: Network Security

Network security stands as the sentinel guarding our invaluable data and infrastructure against the cyber threats. From financial institutions to healthcare providers, from government agencies to small businesses, the importance of robust network security cannot be overstated.

Consider the 2014 cyber-attack on JPMorgan Chase, one of the largest financial institutions in the world. Hackers breached the bank's network, compromising the data of 83 million customers. The repercussions were severe, with stolen personal information fueling identity theft and financial fraud. This incident underscored the critical need for fortified network defenses within the financial sector. Institutions like JPMorgan Chase have since invested significantly in advanced security measures, including robust encryption protocols, multi-factor authentication, and real-time threat monitoring. These efforts have not only bolstered their resilience against cyber threats but also fostered greater trust among their clientele. Even the most stringent regulations like HIPAA can falter in the face of sophisticated cyber-attacks. Take, for instance, the WannaCry ransomware attack in 2017, which targeted healthcare organizations worldwide, including Britain's National Health Service (NHS). The ransomware encrypted vital patient records, disrupting medical services and jeopardizing patient care. This incident served as a wake-up call for the healthcare industry to fortify its network defenses.

Securing Network Infrastructure

A protected network infrastructure is paramount for any organization, especially large enterprises handling sensitive data and serving countless users. A robust defense architecture forms the cornerstone of effective network security. This involves implementing multiple layers of defense mechanisms to thwart potential intrusions. Key components of a comprehensive defense architecture include:

Perimeter Security: Perimeter defenses, such as firewalls, intrusion detection systems (IDS), and intrusion prevention systems (IPS), serve as the first line of defense against external threats. These technologies filter incoming and outgoing traffic, blocking malicious packets and enforcing security policies.

Network Segmentation:
Divide the network into smaller, isolated segments to contain potential breaches and limit the spread of malware or unauthorized access. Employing VLANs (Virtual Local Area Networks) and access controls help enforce segmentation, enhancing overall network security.

Network Protocols and Services

Network protocols and services serve as the backbone of communication within a network. However, they also present potential vulnerabilities that attackers can exploit. It is important to build network security focused on mitigation:

Secure Sockets Layer/Transport Layer Security (SSL/TLS): SSL/TLS protocols encrypt data transmitted over the network, ensuring confidentiality and integrity. Security engineers should configure SSL/TLS settings appropriately, patch known vulnerabilities, and monitor for SSL/TLS-based attacks, such as man-in-the-middle (MITM) attacks. These certificates are issued by trusted Certificate Authorities like DigiCert

Domain Name System (DNS) Security : DNS plays a crucial role in translating domain names into IP addresses, facilitating communication between devices on the internet. DNS security mechanisms,

such as DNSSEC and DNS filtering, help prevent
DNS-based attacks, including cache poisoning, DNS
spoofing, and DNS amplification.

Secure Shell (SSH) Protocol : SSH provides secure
remote access to network devices and servers,
allowing administrators to manage systems remotely.
Security engineers should implement best practices
for SSH configuration, including key-based
authentication, strong ciphers, and access controls to
prevent unauthorized access. Using Privileged
Access Management (PAM) softwares such as
CyberArk, Hashicorp Boundary, Okta, BeyondTrust
can ensure safe access.

Virtual Private Networks:

Large enterprises often utilize VPNs to establish
secure, encrypted connections over the internet,
allowing remote employees to access corporate
resources securely. Implementing VPNs ensures
data privacy and integrity, particularly when
accessing sensitive information from outside the
corporate network.

Network Peering Security

Network peering refers to the arrangement where two
separate internet networks connect and exchange
traffic directly without the need for intermediaries.
Rather than routing traffic through third-party
networks, peering allows direct exchange at peering
points or internet exchange points (IXPs). Peering
typically occurs between Internet Service Providers
(ISPs), Content Delivery Networks (CDNs), cloud
providers, and other large-scale network operators.
Network peering is useful for several reasons:

Improved Performance: By exchanging traffic directly at peering points, networks can reduce latency and improve overall performance for end users. This direct connection often results in faster data transfer speeds and reduced network congestion.

Cost Savings: Peering allows networks to exchange traffic without incurring the costs associated with routing through third-party networks or transit providers. This can lead to significant cost savings for network operators, particularly for high-traffic routes.

Increased Reliability: Direct peering connections offer more reliable and predictable routing paths compared to routing through multiple intermediaries. This can enhance network stability and reduce the risk of disruptions or outages.

The benefits of peering comes with certain security challenges that requires attention.

Unauthorized Access: One of the primary concerns in network peering is the risk of unauthorized access. Without proper authentication and access controls, malicious actors could exploit peering connections to gain unauthorized entry into network infrastructures. Implement strong authentication mechanisms, such as digital certificates or pre-shared keys, to verify the identity of peering partners before establishing connections.

Data Integrity and Interception: Peered networks transmit data packets between each other, raising concerns about interception and eavesdropping. Without encryption mechanisms in place, sensitive information could be intercepted and compromised during transit. Employ cryptographic hashing algorithms or Message Authentication Codes (MACs) to verify the integrity of data packets exchanged between peered networks, ensuring they have not been tampered with during transit.

Denial of Service (DoS) Attacks: Peering connections are susceptible to DoS attacks aimed at disrupting network traffic. Malicious entities could flood peering links with excessive traffic, leading to service degradation or complete outages. Deploy firewalls, IDS/IPS to monitor and filter traffic mitigating malicious activities in real-time.

Routing Security: BGP (Border Gateway Protocol), the protocol used for routing between autonomous systems, is vulnerable to various attacks, including route hijacking and route leaks. Ensuring the authenticity and integrity of routing updates is essential to prevent these types of attacks. Utilize Route Origin Validation (ROV) and BGP prefix filtering to validate the legitimacy of routing updates and prevent route hijacking or leaks.

Chapter 5: Endpoint Security

Endpoint security refers to the protection of individual devices, such as laptops, desktops, smartphones, and tablets, that connect to a corporate network. These endpoints serve as gateways to organizational data and are therefore prime targets for cyber attacks. Endpoint security solutions encompass a range of technologies and strategies designed to detect, prevent, and remediate threats at the device level.

With the proliferation of remote work and the rise of sophisticated cyber threats, endpoints have become increasingly vulnerable targets. A breach at the endpoint can lead to consequences, including data theft, financial loss, and reputational damage. Moreover, compliance regulations such as GDPR and CCPA mandate organizations to implement robust endpoint security measures to protect sensitive information and ensure regulatory compliance.

Endpoint security should be implemented across all devices that connect to the corporate network, including company-owned and BYOD (Bring Your Own Device) endpoints. This encompasses office workstations, laptops, mobile devices, and remote endpoints accessing the network via VPN connections. Additionally, cloud-based endpoint security solutions extend protection to virtualized environments and remote workforce, ensuring comprehensive coverage across all endpoints.

Endpoint Protection Platforms (EPP)

Endpoint Protection Platforms (EPPs) have emerged as a critical component of a comprehensive cybersecurity strategy, providing advanced security features designed to safeguard endpoints such as desktops, laptops, smartphones, and other internet-connected devices. As a security engineer, understanding the intricacies of EPPs and how to effectively operate them is paramount in defending against an array of cyber threats.

Configuring the EPP involves fine-tuning security settings and policies to align with the organization's risk profile and compliance requirements. Security engineers must configure parameters such as firewall rules, antivirus scans, intrusion detection/prevention systems, and data loss prevention mechanisms. Granular controls allow for customized policies tailored to different user groups or departments, enhancing overall security posture.

In the event of a security incident or breach, the EPP facilitates swift response actions to contain the threat and mitigate potential damage. Automated response capabilities such as quarantine, remediation, and rollback enable rapid containment of malicious activity. Security engineers can leverage threat intelligence feeds and forensic tools integrated into the EPP to conduct in-depth investigations and gather evidence for incident response and forensic analysis.

Here's how EPPs ease life for security engineers:

Centralized Management: EPPs offer centralized management consoles that provide a unified view of endpoint security posture and streamline administrative tasks. Security engineers can manage policies, deploy updates, and investigate incidents from a single interface, saving time and effort.

Automation and Orchestration: Automated deployment, configuration, and response capabilities reduce the manual workload on security teams and improve operational efficiency.

Orchestration features enable seamless integration with other security tools and systems, creating a cohesive defense ecosystem.

Proactive Threat Detection: EPPs leverage advanced threat intelligence and behavioral analytics to proactively detect and mitigate security threats before they escalate into full-blown breaches. Real-time alerts and actionable insights empower security engineers to respond promptly to emerging threats, minimizing potential damage.

The landscape of endpoint security is continuously evolving in response to emerging threats, technological advancements, and shifting IT paradigms. Several trends are shaping the future of Endpoint Protection Platforms:

Integration of Artificial Intelligence and Machine Learning : EPP vendors are increasingly leveraging AI and machine learning algorithms to enhance threat detection accuracy, automate response actions, and adapt to evolving threat landscapes.

Zero Trust Architecture: The adoption of Zero Trust principles is driving the evolution of EPPs towards more granular access controls, continuous authentication, and dynamic policy enforcement to mitigate insider threats and lateral movement of attackers.

Cloud-Native and SaaS Solutions: With the proliferation of cloud computing and remote workforces, EPP vendors are developing cloud-native and SaaS-based solutions that offer scalability, agility, and centralized management across distributed environments.

Convergence with EDR and XDR: The convergence of Endpoint Protection Platforms with Endpoint Detection and Response (EDR) and Extended Detection and Response (XDR) solutions is blurring the boundaries between prevention and detection/response capabilities, enabling more holistic and integrated security approaches.

Mobile Device Management (MDM)

Mobile Device Management (MDM) refers to the process of controlling, monitoring, and securing mobile devices such as smartphones, tablets, and laptops deployed across an organization. It encompasses a range of technologies and policies aimed at managing device usage, enforcing security protocols, and ensuring compliance with organizational standards. MDM solutions provide administrators with centralized control over mobile devices, allowing them to configure settings, deploy applications, and enforce security policies remotely. Key Components of Mobile Device Management:

Device Enrollment and Provisioning: MDM platforms facilitate the seamless enrollment of devices into the corporate network, streamlining the onboarding process for new employees or devices. Through automated provisioning, administrators can configure device settings, install necessary applications, and enforce security policies without manual intervention.

Policy Management: MDM solutions enable administrators to define and enforce security policies tailored to the organization's requirements. These policies may include password requirements, encryption settings, application whitelisting/blacklisting, and remote wipe capabilities. By centrally managing policies, administrators can ensure consistency and compliance across all managed devices.

Remote Management and Monitoring: MDM platforms offer robust capabilities for remote management and monitoring of mobile devices. Administrators can remotely troubleshoot issues, track device usage, and monitor compliance with security policies in real-time. This granular visibility allows organizations to proactively address security threats and ensure the integrity of their mobile fleet.

Application Management: With the proliferation of mobile applications, organizations must exercise control over the apps installed on corporate devices. MDM solutions enable administrators to manage app distribution, enforce usage restrictions, and facilitate secure app updates. By maintaining oversight of application usage, organizations can mitigate the risk of malware infections and data breaches.

Security Compliance and Reporting: MDM platforms provide comprehensive reporting capabilities to track device compliance with security policies and regulatory requirements. These reports offer insights into device status, security incidents, and compliance trends, enabling organizations to identify potential vulnerabilities and take proactive measures to mitigate risks.

Remote Desktop Protocol (RDP) Security

Remote Desktop Protocol (RDP) is a proprietary protocol developed by Microsoft, designed to facilitate remote desktop connections between computers. It allows users to access and control a remote computer as if they were physically present at the machine. RDP operates over the Transmission Control Protocol (TCP) port 3389, utilizing encryption to secure communication between client and server. Despite its utility, RDP introduces several security risks that demand attention from security engineers:

Brute Force Attacks: RDP servers are susceptible to brute force attacks, where adversaries repeatedly attempt to guess usernames and passwords to gain unauthorized access.

Denial of Service (DoS) Attacks: Malicious actors can overwhelm RDP servers with a barrage of connection requests, causing service disruptions and potentially rendering systems inaccessible.

Man-in-the-Middle (MitM) Attacks: Without proper encryption and authentication mechanisms, RDP sessions are vulnerable to interception by attackers positioned between the client and server, enabling eavesdropping or data manipulation.

Credential Theft: Weak or reused passwords pose a significant threat, as attackers can intercept credentials during RDP authentication or exploit compromised credentials to infiltrate systems.

Chapter 6: Cloud Security with AWS

In the digital landscape of the 21st century, the proliferation of cloud computing has revolutionized the way businesses operate, data is stored, and services are delivered. Cloud technology offers unprecedented scalability, flexibility, and accessibility, empowering organizations to streamline their operations and innovate at a rapid pace. However, as the reliance on cloud services grows, so too does the need to address the critical issue of cloud security. Ensuring the confidentiality, integrity, and availability of data in the cloud has become paramount, as cyber threats continue to evolve in sophistication and scale.

Cloud computing has evolved from a mere buzzword to a foundational technology that underpins the digital transformation of businesses across industries. Traditional on-premises infrastructure, with its inherent limitations in scalability and agility, has been gradually supplanted by cloud solutions offered by tech giants such as Amazon Web Services (AWS), Microsoft Azure, and Google Cloud Platform (GCP). The cloud's ability to provide on-demand access to computing resources, storage, and applications has fueled its widespread adoption, enabling organizations to harness the power of data analytics, artificial intelligence, and machine learning to drive innovation and gain competitive advantage.

While the benefits of cloud computing are undeniable, the shared responsibility model inherent in cloud environments introduces unique security challenges. Unlike traditional IT infrastructure where security measures are primarily managed in-house, cloud security requires collaboration between cloud service providers (CSPs) and their customers. CSPs are responsible for securing the underlying infrastructure, network, and physical data centers, while customers are tasked with securing their data, applications, and user access within the cloud environment. This division of responsibility underscores the importance of implementing robust security measures to protect against a myriad of threats, including data breaches, malware, insider threats, and denial-of-service (DoS) attacks.

With the implementation of stringent data protection regulations such as the General Data Protection Regulation (GDPR) and the California Consumer Privacy Act (CCPA), organizations face increased pressure to safeguard the privacy of sensitive information stored in the cloud. Failure to comply with these regulations can result in hefty fines, legal repercussions, and irreparable damage to reputation. Cloud security measures such as encryption, access controls, and data masking play a crucial role in ensuring compliance with regulatory requirements and maintaining the trust of customers and stakeholders.

The global shift towards remote work in the wake of the COVID-19 pandemic has further underscored the importance of cloud security. With employees accessing corporate resources from diverse locations and devices, the traditional perimeter-based security model is no longer sufficient to protect against emerging threats. Cloud-based security solutions such as virtual private networks (VPNs), multi-factor authentication (MFA), and secure web gateways (SWGs) are essential for securing remote workforces and preventing unauthorized access to sensitive data.

In an era of increasingly sophisticated cyber attacks, proactive threat intelligence is essential for identifying and mitigating emerging threats before they escalate into full-blown security incidents. Cloud security platforms leverage advanced analytics, machine learning, and artificial intelligence to analyze vast amounts of data and detect anomalous behavior indicative of potential security breaches. By continuously monitoring cloud environments for suspicious activity and vulnerabilities, organizations can strengthen their security posture and preemptively respond to threats in real-time.

Among the leading providers in this domain stands Amazon Web Services (AWS), offering a plethora of services designed to enhance efficiency and scalability. Here are some essential strategies for implementing effective cloud security:

Identity and Access Management (IAM): Implement robust IAM policies to control access to cloud resources based on user roles, privileges, and authentication mechanisms. Through IAM, administrators can create custom policies, define roles, and grant granular access permissions, thereby enforcing the principle of least privilege.

Encryption: Data encryption plays a pivotal role in safeguarding sensitive information from unauthorized access or interception. AWS offers a myriad of encryption services, including AWS Key

35

Management Service (KMS) for managing encryption keys, AWS CloudHSM for hardware-based key storage, and AWS Certificate Manager for securing communication through SSL/TLS certificates. Employing encryption at rest and in transit ensures end-to-end protection, mitigating risks associated with data breaches or malicious activities.

Network Security: Implement network segmentation, firewalls, and intrusion detection and prevention systems (IDPS) to protect against unauthorized network access and malicious activities. Virtual Private Cloud (VPC) enables customers to create isolated network environments, complete with custom IP addressing, subnets, and route tables. Network Access Control Lists (NACLs) and Security Groups further bolster security by filtering traffic at the subnet and instance level, respectively, based on user-defined rulesets. Additionally, AWS Web Application Firewall (WAF) safeguards web applications from common exploits and attacks, such as SQL injection and cross-site scripting (XSS).

Compliance and Governance: Compliance and governance frameworks serve as essential pillars of cloud security. AWS offers a comprehensive suite of compliance certifications, including SOC 1/2/3, PCI DSS, HIPAA, and GDPR, attesting its commitment to adhering to industry best practices and regulatory mandates. AWS Config and AWS Organizations facilitate governance by enabling continuous monitoring, auditing, and policy enforcement across AWS accounts and resources.

Security Monitoring and Incident Response: Despite robust preventive measures, security incidents may still occur, necessitating a swift and effective response mechanism. AWS provides a plethora of monitoring and logging services, such as Amazon

CloudWatch, AWS CloudTrail, and Amazon GuardDuty, enabling real-time detection of suspicious activities, unauthorized access attempts, and compliance violations. Leveraging automated response mechanisms, such as AWS Lambda functions or AWS Config Rules, enhances incident response capabilities, enabling organizations to mitigate security threats proactively.

Securing Cloud Infrastructure

With the advent of Infrastructure as a Service (IaaS), Platform as a Service (PaaS), and Function as a Service (FaaS), the landscape of IT infrastructure has evolved significantly. Among the leading cloud service providers, Amazon Web Services (AWS) stands out with its Elastic Compute Cloud (EC2), container services, and serverless offerings. However, as organizations increasingly rely on these cloud services, ensuring the security of cloud workloads becomes paramount.

EC2 instances form the backbone of many cloud deployments, providing scalable compute capacity. However, leaving EC2 instances unsecured can expose organizations to a plethora of risks. Some best practices for securing EC2 instances:

Least Privilege Access: Implement the principle of least privilege by granting only necessary permissions to EC2 instances. Utilize IAM roles and policies to create restricted accesses.

Network Security: Leverage security groups and network access control lists (ACLs) to control inbound and outbound traffic to EC2 instances. Implement strict ingress and egress rules to limit exposure to potential threats.

Patch Management: Regularly update EC2 instances with the latest security patches to address vulnerabilities. Utilize AWS Systems Manager or third-party patch management solutions to automate patching processes.

Encryption: Encrypt data at rest and in transit to protect sensitive information. Utilize AWS Key Management Service (KMS) to manage encryption keys and enforce encryption for EBS volumes and data transferred over the network.

Monitoring and Logging: Implement comprehensive logging and monitoring solutions to track activities and detect anomalies. Utilize Amazon CloudWatch Logs, AWS CloudTrail, and third-party monitoring tools to gain visibility into EC2 instance activity.

Container Management

Containers have gained popularity for their lightweight, portable, and scalable nature. However, securing containerized workloads requires specialized considerations. Here are key security best practices for container deployments:

Image Security: Use trusted base images from reputable sources and regularly scan container images for vulnerabilities. Implement image signing and verification mechanisms to ensure the integrity of images.

Container Isolation: Utilize container orchestration platforms like Amazon Elastic Kubernetes Service (EKS) or Amazon Elastic Container Service (ECS) to enforce isolation between containers. Implement pod security policies and network policies to restrict container-to-container communication.

Secrets Management: Safely manage sensitive information such as API keys, passwords, and certificates using secret management solutions like AWS Secrets Manager or HashiCorp Vault. Avoid hardcoding secrets within container images or configuration files.

Serverless Computing

Serverless computing, exemplified by AWS Lambda, offers a serverless execution environment for running code without provisioning or managing servers. Despite its benefits, securing serverless functions presents unique challenges. Here's how to enhance serverless function security.

Function Isolation: Leverage AWS Lambda's execution environment to isolate serverless functions from each other. Implement resource policies to restrict function access to specific AWS resources.

Input Validation: Validate input data to serverless functions to prevent injection attacks and ensure data integrity. Implement input validation and sanitization mechanisms to filter out malicious input.

Function Permissions: Assign appropriate IAM roles to serverless functions to restrict access to AWS resources based on the principle of least privilege. Avoid overly permissive IAM policies that grant unnecessary permissions.

Cloud Workload Orchestration

Managing cloud workloads involves orchestrating diverse resources across EC2 instances, containers, and serverless functions. Here are strategies for effectively managing cloud workloads while prioritizing security:

Automation and Orchestration: Leverage infrastructure as code (IaC) tools such as AWS CloudFormation or Terraform to automate provisioning and configuration management of cloud resources. Implement CI/CD pipelines to ensure consistent deployment and configuration across environments.

DevSecOps Integration: Embed security practices into the development and deployment pipeline through DevSecOps integration. Integrate security testing, vulnerability scanning, and compliance checks into CI/CD workflows to identify and remediate security issues early in the development lifecycle.

Continuous Compliance: Implement continuous compliance monitoring to ensure cloud workloads adhere to security policies and regulatory requirements. Utilize AWS Config Rules and third-party compliance automation tools to evaluate resource configurations against predefined security baselines.

Chapter 7: Application Security

Application security refers to the measures taken to protect software applications from threats or attacks throughout their lifecycle. It encompasses various processes, tools, and methodologies aimed at identifying, mitigating, and preventing vulnerabilities that could compromise the confidentiality, integrity, or availability of data and systems. Unlike network or infrastructure security, which focuses on protecting the perimeter, application security concentrates on safeguarding the software itself from both internal and external threats.

Implementation Strategies for Application Security

Secure Coding Practices: Developers should adhere to secure coding guidelines, such as those outlined by OWASP (Open Web Application Security Project), to mitigate common vulnerabilities such as injection attacks, insecure deserialization, and broken authentication.

Security Testing: Regular security testing, including static analysis, dynamic analysis, and penetration testing, should be conducted throughout the development lifecycle to identify and remediate vulnerabilities.

Secure Configuration Management: Proper configuration of application servers, databases, and other components is essential to minimize the risk of misconfigurations that could lead to security breaches.

Access Controls: Implement robust authentication and authorization mechanisms to ensure that only authorized users have access to sensitive data and functionality within the application.

Encryption and Data Protection: Utilize encryption to protect sensitive data both in transit and at rest, and implement secure data handling practices to prevent data leakage or unauthorized access.

Application API Security

API security encompasses a set of measures and protocols designed to safeguard the integrity, confidentiality, and availability of APIs and the data they handle. It involves protecting against unauthorized access, data breaches, injection attacks, and other malicious activities that could compromise the security posture of both the API provider and its consumers. Effective API security strategies encompass various layers, including authentication, authorization, encryption, input validation, rate limiting, and monitoring.

Common API Security Threats:

Unauthorized Access:

Unauthorized access occurs when attackers exploit weaknesses in authentication mechanisms to gain unauthorized entry to APIs and sensitive data. Weak or leaked API keys, compromised credentials, and broken authentication workflows are common vectors for unauthorized access attacks.

Injection Attacks:

Injection attacks involve injecting malicious payloads into API requests to manipulate application logic, execute arbitrary code, or access unauthorized data. SQL injection, NoSQL injection, and command injection are prevalent injection attack vectors that can lead to data breaches and service disruption.

Broken Authentication:

Broken authentication vulnerabilities arise from flawed authentication and session management practices, enabling attackers to hijack user sessions, impersonate legitimate users, or bypass access controls. Common issues include weak passwords, session fixation, and insecure token handling.

Data Exposure:

Data exposure occurs when APIs inadvertently expose sensitive information such as personally identifiable information (PII), financial data, or authentication tokens to unauthorized parties. Inadequate encryption, improper data handling, and insufficient access controls contribute to data exposure risks.

Denial-of-Service (DoS) Attacks:

Denial-of-Service (DoS) attacks target API endpoints with an overwhelming volume of requests, causing service degradation or outage. Distributed Denial-of-Service (DDoS) attacks amplify the impact by coordinating attack traffic from multiple sources, making it challenging to differentiate legitimate requests from malicious ones.

Chapter 8: Managing secrets with secret managers

What Constitutes a Secret?

At its core, a secret encapsulates information that is intended to be concealed from unauthorized access. This clandestine nature imbues secrets with immense significance, as they serve as the linchpin of numerous security protocols and mechanisms. Cryptographic keys, passwords, API tokens, and encryption algorithms are quintessential examples of secrets that safeguard sensitive data, systems, and communications. Rather than dispersing credentials across disparate systems and applications, secrets managers consolidate this information into a single, easily manageable platform. Centralized management streamlines operations, enhances visibility, and facilitates more effective auditing and compliance efforts.

Despite their pivotal role, secrets are not immutable entities; they are subject to constant evolution and management. The landscape of secrets management is multifaceted, encompassing processes for generation, storage, distribution, rotation, and revocation. Security engineers are tasked with orchestrating these intricate maneuvers, ensuring that secrets remain shielded from prying eyes while facilitating legitimate access for authorized entities.

The Risks of Poor Secrets Management

The ramifications of lapses in secrets management reverberate far beyond mere inconvenience; they can precipitate catastrophic breaches with enduring consequences. A fundamental risk associated with poor secrets management is unauthorized access, wherein malicious actors exploit compromised secrets to infiltrate systems, exfiltrate sensitive data, or orchestrate destructive attacks. Furthermore, the proliferation of secrets across disparate platforms and repositories amplifies the complexity of management, escalating the likelihood of inadvertent exposure or misconfiguration.

Another peril lies in the realm of compliance and regulatory frameworks, where stringent mandates dictate the safeguarding of confidential information. Organizations that fail to adhere to these stipulations face severe penalties, tarnished reputations, and legal repercussions. Moreover, the erosion of trust among users can inflict irreparable damage to brand integrity, precipitating a cascade of detrimental consequences for the business ecosystem.

In addition to external threats, internal vulnerabilities pose a formidable challenge to secrets management. Human fallibility, manifested through negligence, oversight, or malicious intent, can catalyze breaches from within the organization's ranks. The absence of robust access controls, insufficient auditing mechanisms, and inadequate training exacerbate these vulnerabilities, laying bare the underbelly of the security infrastructure to exploitation.

Key Features and Capabilities

Secrets managers provide a secure repository for storing sensitive information such as passwords, API keys, cryptographic keys, and tokens. These repositories are often encrypted to ensure that data remains protected both at rest and in transit. Advanced encryption algorithms and cryptographic protocols bolster the security posture, thwarting unauthorized access attempts.

Encryption and cryptographic algorithms:
AES (Advanced Encryption Standard): AES is a symmetric encryption algorithm widely used for securing data. It supports key lengths of 128, 192, or 256 bits. Popular Secrets Management softwares in the market like AWS Secrets Manager, Hashicorp Vault, CyberArk uses AES encryption algorithms to store secrets.
RSA (Rivest-Shamir-Adleman): RSA is an asymmetric encryption algorithm commonly used for secure key exchange and digital signatures. It relies on the practical difficulty of factoring large prime numbers. RSA is widely used in digital certificates, such as SSL certificates.
ECDSA (Elliptic Curve Digital Signature Algorithm): ECDSA is another asymmetric algorithm, particularly well-suited for environments with constrained

resources (e.g., mobile devices, IoT devices). It operates on elliptic curve cryptography.

PBKDF2 (Password-Based Key Derivation Function 2): PBKDF2 is a key derivation function that strengthens passwords against brute-force attacks by applying cryptographic hash functions iteratively.

Argon2: Argon2 is a memory-hard key derivation function that provides resistance against GPU and ASIC attacks. It's specifically designed for password hashing.

Access Control:

Secrets managers enforce robust access controls to regulate who can access sensitive information and under what circumstances. Granular access policies enable security engineers to define roles, permissions, and authentication mechanisms, ensuring that only authorized individuals can retrieve or modify secrets. Role-based access control (RBAC) frameworks further enhance security by aligning access privileges with job responsibilities.

Access policies define the permissions granted to users, groups, or services at a more granular level. These policies specify which actions are allowed or denied for specific secrets or resource types. Policies can be written in a language specific to the Secrets Manager or using a standardized format such as JSON or YAML.

Secrets Manager often integrates with various authentication mechanisms to verify the identity of users or services accessing the secrets. This can include username/password authentication, API keys, OAuth tokens, or integration with identity providers like AWS IAM, Azure Active Directory, or Google Identity Platform.

Rotation and Lifecycle Management:

To mitigate the risk of credential exposure and unauthorized access, secrets managers incorporate automated rotation and lifecycle management functionalities. These features enable security engineers to periodically rotate credentials, such as passwords and keys, based on predefined policies. Automated rotation reduces the window of vulnerability and minimizes the impact of potential security breaches.

Auditing and Logging:

Detailed audit logs capture information such as who accessed which secrets, when the access occurred, and from which IP address. Auditing logs can hold users accountable for their actions by documenting their activities within the secrets manager, discouraging malicious behavior and promoting responsible use.

Additionally, audit logs can show successful and failed authentication attempts, indicating potential security threats or misconfigurations in access control policies. Logging mechanisms can record errors, exceptions, and warnings encountered during operations, helping in troubleshooting issues and ensuring system reliability.

By maintaining a chronological record of activities, these logs facilitate forensic analysis, compliance reporting, and incident response efforts. Analyzing audit logs can help in identifying unusual access patterns or behavior deviations, indicating potential security breaches or insider threats.

Strategies for Multi-Cloud Environments

In multi-cloud environments, where businesses utilize services and resources from multiple cloud providers, managing secrets securely becomes increasingly complex. When you're dealing with multiple cloud services, handling lots of different native secrets managers for passwords and sensitive data can be a real headache. Instead of having to track down each secrets manager separately just to change secrets or keep track of who's accessed what, a centralized secrets management system gives you one place to do it all.

Independent and Centralized Secret Managers: Utilize a centralized secrets management tool that supports multi-cloud environments. Some popular options include HashiCorp Vault, Akeyless, CyberArk, Doppler.

Cross-Cloud Replication: If possible, replicate secrets across multiple cloud providers for redundancy and fault tolerance. This helps mitigate the risk of data loss due to outages or failures in a single cloud environment.

Blockchain-based Secrets Management

Traditional methods of secrets management, such as storing credentials in centralized repositories or relying on encryption keys, are no longer sufficient in mitigating the evolving threats posed by malicious actors. Blockchain technology can be used to create a decentralized, immutable ledger system that offers a paradigm shift in secrets management.

Secrets are encrypted and stored as transactions on the blockchain, with each transaction cryptographically linked to the previous one to maintain the integrity of the ledger. Access to secrets is controlled through cryptographic keys, which are securely stored and managed by authorized users or applications.

Immutable Ledger: One of the fundamental principles of blockchain technology is immutability. Each transaction or data entry recorded on the blockchain is cryptographically linked to the previous one, creating an unchangeable and transparent ledger. In the context of secrets management, this means that once a secret is stored on the blockchain, it cannot be altered or tampered with by unauthorized parties. This inherent security feature provides a robust defense against data manipulation and unauthorized access, enhancing the integrity and reliability of secrets management systems.

Decentralization: Traditional secrets management systems often rely on centralized repositories or third-party providers to store sensitive information. However, centralized systems are vulnerable to single points of failure and are attractive targets for cyber attacks. By leveraging blockchain technology, secrets can be distributed across a decentralized network of nodes, eliminating the need for a central authority and reducing the risk of data breaches. Each node in the blockchain network maintains a copy of the ledger, ensuring redundancy and resilience against attacks aimed at compromising the system.

Enhanced Security: Blockchain-based secrets management utilizes cryptographic techniques to secure sensitive information. Secrets are encrypted before being stored on the blockchain, ensuring that only authorized parties with the corresponding decryption keys can access them. Additionally, blockchain networks employ consensus mechanisms, such as proof of work or proof of stake, to validate and authenticate transactions. This adds an extra layer of security by preventing unauthorized modifications to the ledger and ensuring that only legitimate transactions are accepted.

Rehide is one such secrets manager that is based on blockchain-based secrets management solution in the market.

Chapter 9: Detect and secure leaked secrets

Sprawled secrets refer to sensitive information scattered across various digital assets within an organization's network or publicly on internet. These secrets encompass a wide range of critical data, including passwords, cryptographic keys, API tokens, and other authentication credentials. The proliferation of sprawled secrets can occur due to various factors, including inadequate security practices, poor access controls, and the proliferation of cloud-based services.

Given the covert nature of sprawled secrets, detecting their presence within an organization's ecosystem necessitates a multifaceted approach combining automated tools, proactive monitoring, and rigorous auditing practices. Security engineers can leverage specialized tools like credential scanners, static code analysis tools, and configuration management platforms to conduct comprehensive scans of code repositories, infrastructure configurations, and container images for potential exposure of secrets. Additionally, implementing robust logging and monitoring solutions enables real-time detection of anomalous activities indicative of unauthorized access attempts to sensitive information.

By establishing a centralized repository for secrets management and enforcing strict access controls, security teams can mitigate the risk of sprawled secrets and enhance visibility into their organization's security posture.

Impact of Leaked Secrets:

The ramifications of a leaked secret hotspot extend far beyond individual inconvenience. From a corporate perspective, the exposure of sensitive information through an unsecured network can result in significant financial losses, reputational damage, and legal liabilities. Moreover, the exploitation of such vulnerabilities can serve as a foothold for attackers to infiltrate internal systems, leading to data breaches, service disruptions, and even industrial espionage.

Secret leak hotspots in Enterprises:

Source Code Repositories :

Developers, in their haste or oversight, may embed secrets directly into the code, inadvertently exposing them to prying eyes during version control commits. They can be found in configuration files, code comments, or hardcoded strings. Even if secrets are removed from the latest commit, they may still exist in the repository's history. Tools like git log and git diff can be used to inspect previous commits and identify any inadvertently committed secrets.

In addition to internal repositories, organizations may rely on third-party libraries or dependencies hosted on platforms like GitHub or Bitbucket. These external repositories can also contain leaked secrets, either intentionally or unintentionally disclosed by their contributors.

Git based version control systems offer Git Hooks. Pre-commit and pre-receive git hooks can be used to enforce policies that prevent the inadvertent inclusion of secrets in commits pushed to the repository.

These hooks can trigger automated checks or reject commits containing potential secrets. Using scanning tools that support git hooks is essential.

Application Binaries and Artifacts:
During the build process, sensitive information may inadvertently get embedded into the final application binaries or intermediate artifacts. These artifacts, if not properly sanitized, can inadvertently expose secrets. In runtime environments, secrets may reside temporarily in memory. Memory dumps, whether intentional or accidental, can expose these secrets to potential attackers.

Container Images and Registries:
Containerization has revolutionized software development, offering scalability, portability, and efficiency. However, with this convenience comes a new set of security concerns, particularly regarding the protection of sensitive information such as secrets.

Build-Time Leaks: During the build process, developers may inadvertently embed secrets directly into the container image. This could occur due to hardcoded values or misconfigured build scripts.

Runtime Leaks: Secrets may also be exposed at runtime if not properly managed within the container environment. Vulnerabilities in application code or misconfigured environment variables can lead to the inadvertent exposure of sensitive information.

Third-Party Dependencies: Container images often rely on third-party libraries and dependencies. If these dependencies contain vulnerabilities or hardcoded secrets, they can serve as potential entry points for attackers.

In 2018, Tesla suffered a breach due to misconfigured Docker containers containing AWS credentials. Attackers exploited these leaked credentials to mine cryptocurrency, resulting in substantial financial losses for the company.

Public container registries like Docker Hub are treasure troves for attackers seeking leaked secrets. These repositories host millions of container images, making them prime targets for malicious actors scouring for vulnerabilities. Container images are typically built in layers, with each layer representing a specific component or configuration. Leaked secrets may be embedded within these layers, hidden amidst the filesystem or configuration files.

Instant messaging tools and integrations:
Instant messaging platforms have revolutionized communication within organizations, facilitating quick exchanges and collaboration among team members. However, this convenience comes with inherent security risks, particularly in terms of safeguarding sensitive information. As a security engineer, it is crucial to understand where to find secret leaks and how to detect them effectively to mitigate potential threats.

Chats: Instant messaging platforms like Slack, Microsoft Teams, and Discord offer various channels or chat rooms for different teams or projects. These channels often become hotspots for sharing sensitive information, inadvertently exposing it to unauthorized individuals. While direct messages are intended for private conversations, they can still pose a rlsk if sensitive information is exchanged. Many instant messaging platforms allow users to share files directly within chats. These files may contain confidential documents, financial records, or proprietary information that could be leaked if not adequately secured.

Integration with Third-Party Apps: Integration with third-party applications can expand the functionality of instant messaging platforms but also increases the surface area for potential security vulnerabilities. Unauthorized access to these integrations could result in the leakage of sensitive data.

One of the primary methods of detecting leaked secrets is through rigorous analysis of message content. Security engineers can employ advanced algorithms and machine learning techniques to scan messages for patterns indicative of sensitive information. Keywords such as "confidential," "password," "proprietary," or specific project names can serve as red flags warranting further investigation.

By scrutinizing user behavior within instant messaging platforms, security engineers can identify anomalies that may signify a data breach. Unusual patterns of communication, sudden spikes in file transfers, or access from unrecognized devices are all indicators that merit immediate attention.

Third-Party Libraries and Dependencies:

The reliance on third-party libraries and dependencies has become ubiquitous. These libraries offer developers a shortcut to integrate complex functionalities, accelerating the development process. While developers may overlook vulnerabilities in third party libraries during integration, threat actors keenly exploit them to gain unauthorized access or orchestrate cyber attacks. Consequently, the onus falls on security engineers to proactively identify and remediate such weaknesses before they are exploited.

Cloud Storage buckets:

Cloud storage buckets serve as repositories for various types of data, ranging from documents and images to configuration files and encryption keys. These buckets are typically hosted by cloud service providers such as Amazon Web Services (AWS), Google Cloud Platform (GCP), and Microsoft Azure. While these platforms offer robust security features, misconfigurations or lax access controls can inadvertently expose sensitive information to unauthorized parties.

As a security engineer, understanding the risks associated with cloud storage and knowing how to detect and prevent leaks of confidential data is paramount.

One common source of leaked secrets is publicly accessible storage buckets. In some cases, organizations inadvertently configure their buckets to allow unrestricted access, making sensitive data accessible to anyone with the URL. Implementing Data Loss Prevention (DLP) solutions can help organizations proactively identify and prevent the unauthorized sharing of sensitive data. These solutions use machine learning algorithms to analyze data patterns and detect anomalies indicative of potential security breaches.

Logs:

Logs are indispensable tools for system administrators and developers, providing a detailed record of activities and events within a system. Many applications generate logs to track user activities, errors, and system events. If developers inadvertently include sensitive information in log statements, these details can be easily accessed.

Logs from application, CI/CD pipelines, and networking tools should be scanned to detect sensitive secrets.

In 2023, attackers targeted Okta's customer support system using a service account credential that an employee had stored in personal google account. They downloaded "HAR" log files containing session recordings of customer support interactions. This included sensitive information entered by customers seeking help. Though Okta alerted all their customers of this attack, attackers were able to attack Okta customers like 1Password, BeyondTrust, Cloudflare etc.. from sensitive log data.

Collaborative Remediation of leaked secrets:

Effective remediation of leaked secrets demands a collaborative approach that leverages the expertise and resources of various stakeholders within an organization. Security engineers play a central role in facilitating this collaboration by establishing clear communication channels, defining roles and responsibilities, and orchestrating remediation workflows. The following framework outlines key steps in the collaborative remediation process:

Detection and Identification:

1. Prompt detection of leaked secrets through continuous monitoring and anomaly detection mechanisms.
2. Thorough investigation to identify the scope and nature of the breach, including affected systems, users, and data.

Containment and Damage Control:

1. Isolation of compromised systems and assets to prevent further unauthorized access.
2. Immediate revocation and replacement of leaked credentials, keys, or tokens to mitigate the risk of exploitation.

Impact Assessment:
1. Assessment of the potential impact of the leak on confidentiality, integrity, and availability of data and services.
2. Evaluation of regulatory compliance implications and notification requirements.

Remediation Planning and Execution:
1. Collaborative development of a remediation plan that prioritizes critical systems and minimizes disruption to operations.
2. Implementation of security patches, configuration changes, and access controls to address underlying vulnerabilities.

Continuous Monitoring and Improvement:
1. Ongoing monitoring of remediation measures to ensure their effectiveness and resilience against future threats.
2. Iterative refinement of security policies, procedures, and technologies based on lessons learned from the incident.

Collaborative remediation of leaked secrets is not without its challenges. Coordination among diverse teams with varying priorities and expertise can be complex, requiring effective communication and leadership from security engineers. Moreover, the time-sensitive nature of remediation efforts necessitates rapid decision-making and prioritization of actions to minimize the impact of the breach. Additionally, organizations must strike a balance between transparency and confidentiality when communicating about security incidents to internal stakeholders, customers, and regulatory authorities.

Chapter 10: Regulatory Compliance and Legal Considerations

Regulatory compliance refers to the adherence to laws, regulations, guidelines, and specifications relevant to a particular industry or jurisdiction. In addition to regulatory compliance, security engineers must navigate a complex web of legal considerations that encompass contractual obligations, liability issues, and emerging legal trends.

Contractual obligations often dictate the terms of engagement between organizations and their clients or service providers. Security engineers must meticulously review and negotiate contracts to ensure that security requirements are clearly defined, responsibilities are allocated appropriately, and compliance obligations are met.

Liability issues loom large in the realm of cybersecurity, particularly in the aftermath of data breaches or security incidents. Security engineers may be held accountable for lapses in security measures or failures to mitigate risks effectively. Understanding the legal framework surrounding liability is essential for security engineers to mitigate potential legal exposure and safeguard their organization's interests.

Emerging legal trends, such as the proliferation of data protection laws and the rise of cybersecurity litigation, further underscore the importance of staying abreast of legal developments. Security engineers must proactively adapt their security strategies to align with evolving legal standards and emerging threats, thereby mitigating legal risks and ensuring compliance with applicable laws and regulations.

The global nature of cyberspace introduces jurisdictional complexities that pose challenges for security engineers. Data privacy laws, regulatory frameworks, and legal standards vary across different countries and regions, necessitating a nuanced understanding of international law. Security engineers must navigate these complexities when designing security protocols, managing cross-border data transfers, and addressing legal requirements in diverse jurisdictions.

Regulations on cybersecurity compliance vary significantly across different countries and regions. Here are some examples of prominent regulations and standards in various parts of the world:

United States:

NIST Cybersecurity Framework: Developed by the National Institute of Standards and Technology (NIST), this framework provides voluntary guidance for managing and reducing cybersecurity risk.

SOC 2: SOC 2 audit reports are intended to provide assurance about the security, availability, processing integrity, confidentiality, and privacy of an organization's systems.

HIPAA (Health Insurance Portability and Accountability Act): Regulates the protection of sensitive patient data in the healthcare industry.

PCI DSS (Payment Card Industry Data Security Standard): Applies to companies that handle credit card payments to ensure the secure processing, storage, and transmission of cardholder data.

GDPR (General Data Protection Regulation): While originating in the EU, GDPR can have implications for U.S. companies that handle EU citizens' data.

European Union:

GDPR (General Data Protection Regulation): One of the most comprehensive data protection regulations globally, governing the processing of personal data of EU residents.

NIS Directive (Network and Information Security Directive): Applies to operators of essential services and digital service providers, requiring them to ensure the security of their network and information systems.

ePrivacy Directive: Focuses on privacy and confidentiality in the electronic communications sector, including requirements for consent and data breach notifications.

Australia:

Privacy Act 1988 (with amendments): Regulates the handling of personal information by Australian government agencies and businesses.

Notifiable Data Breaches (NDB) scheme: Requires organizations to notify affected individuals and the Australian Information Commissioner of eligible data breaches.

National Institute of Standards and Technology (NIST)

NIST is a comprehensive set of guidelines, standards, and best practices designed to help organizations manage and improve their cybersecurity posture. Developed by NIST in response to Executive Order 13636, the framework provides a flexible and risk-based approach to cybersecurity, allowing organizations to assess and strengthen their security capabilities based on their unique needs, risk tolerance, and business objectives.

The Framework Core consists of five concurrent and continuous functions that serve as the foundation for managing and mitigating cybersecurity risks:

a. Identify: Organizations must understand their cybersecurity risks by identifying assets, systems, data, and potential vulnerabilities. This involves establishing governance structures, conducting risk assessments, and developing an inventory of critical assets.

b. Protect: Once risks are identified, organizations must implement safeguards to protect against potential threats. This includes implementing access controls, encryption, security awareness training, and secure configuration management.

c. Detect: Organizations must have capabilities in place to detect cybersecurity events in a timely manner. This involves implementing intrusion detection systems, log monitoring, anomaly detection, and security incident response procedures.

d. Respond: In the event of a cybersecurity incident, organizations must have effective response procedures to mitigate the impact and restore normal operations. This includes incident response planning, communication protocols, and coordination with external stakeholders.

e. Recover: Organizations must have plans and processes in place to recover from cybersecurity incidents and restore systems and data to a secure state. This involves backup and recovery procedures, continuity planning, and post-incident analysis to identify lessons learned and improve resilience.

SOC 2 Compliance

SOC 2 compliance is based on the Trust Services Criteria, which consists of five key principles:
Security: The system is protected against unauthorized access (both physical and logical).
Availability: The system is available for operation and use as committed or agreed.
Processing Integrity: System processing is complete, valid, accurate, timely, and authorized.
Confidentiality: Information designated as confidential is protected as committed or agreed.
Privacy: Personal information is collected, used, retained, disclosed, and disposed of in conformity with the entity's privacy notice, and with criteria set forth in Generally Accepted Privacy Principles (GAPP) issued by the AICPA and Canadian Institute of Chartered Accountants (CICA).
SOC 2 compliance involves a thorough audit of an organization's internal controls and processes related to these principles. It is particularly relevant for service providers that store customer data in the cloud or provide SaaS (Software as a Service) solutions. SOC 2 reports are often requested by customers or partners as a way to assess the security and privacy controls of service providers.
There are two types of SOC 2 reports:
Type I: This report evaluates the suitability and design of the organization's controls at a specific point in time.
Type II: This report provides more detailed information by evaluating the operational effectiveness of the organization's controls over a specified period, typically six to twelve months.

General Data Protection Regulation (GDPR):

General Data Protection Regulation, is a comprehensive data protection and privacy regulation established by the European Union (EU) to strengthen the protection of personal data and privacy for EU citizens. Compliance with GDPR is crucial for organizations that handle the personal data of EU residents, regardless of where the organization is located.

In the context of cybersecurity, GDPR compliance involves implementing measures to protect personal data from unauthorized access, disclosure, alteration, or destruction. Here are some key considerations for GDPR compliance in cybersecurity:

Data Security Measures: GDPR requires organizations to implement appropriate technical and organizational measures to ensure the security of personal data. This includes encryption, access controls, pseudonymization, and regular security assessments to identify and address vulnerabilities.

Data Breach Notification: GDPR mandates organizations to report data breaches to the relevant supervisory authority within 72 hours of becoming aware of the breach, unless the breach is unlikely to result in a risk to the rights and freedoms of individuals. Additionally, organizations must notify affected individuals without undue delay if the breach is likely to result in a high risk to their rights and freedoms.

Privacy by Design and Default: GDPR promotes the concept of privacy by design and default, which means that organizations should integrate data protection and privacy considerations into the design and implementation of their systems, processes, and services from the outset. This includes considering data security measures, data minimization, and user consent mechanisms.

Data Transfer Safeguards: GDPR imposes restrictions on the transfer of personal data outside the European Economic Area (EEA) to ensure an adequate level of protection. Organizations must implement appropriate safeguards, such as standard contractual clauses or binding corporate rules, when transferring personal data to countries without an adequacy decision from the EU Commission.

Data Protection Impact Assessments (DPIAs): GDPR requires organizations to conduct DPIAs for high-risk processing activities that are likely to result in a high risk to individuals' rights and freedoms. DPIAs help organizations identify and mitigate risks to data protection and privacy before implementing new projects or processes.

Vendor Management: Organizations are responsible for ensuring that third-party vendors (processors) who handle personal data on their behalf comply with GDPR requirements. This includes implementing contractual agreements, conducting due diligence on vendors' security practices, and monitoring their compliance.

Health Insurance Portability and Accountability Act (HIPAA)

Health Insurance Portability and Accountability Act, sets forth requirements for protecting sensitive patient health information (PHI) and electronic protected health information (ePHI). While HIPAA is primarily focused on ensuring the privacy and security of healthcare data, it intersects with cybersecurity in several ways:

Data Security Safeguards: HIPAA requires covered entities (such as healthcare providers, health plans, and healthcare clearinghouses) and their business associates (entities that handle PHI on behalf of covered entities) to implement administrative, physical, and technical safeguards to protect ePHI. These safeguards include measures such as access controls, encryption, and secure transmission protocols, all of which are integral components of cybersecurity.

Risk Assessment and Management: HIPAA mandates that covered entities conduct regular risk assessments to identify potential vulnerabilities to the confidentiality, integrity, and availability of ePHI. This process is akin to cybersecurity risk assessments, which help organizations identify and prioritize security threats and vulnerabilities.

Incident Response: HIPAA requires covered entities to have procedures in place for responding to security incidents and breaches involving ePHI. This includes investigating incidents, mitigating risks, and notifying affected individuals, regulators, and other parties as required. Cybersecurity incident response plans are crucial for effectively managing and containing data breaches, and they often align with HIPAA requirements.

Business Associate Agreements (BAAs): Covered entities must enter into BAAs with their business associates to ensure that these third-party entities also comply with HIPAA's privacy and security rules. BAAs typically outline the specific security measures that business associates must implement to protect ePHI, including cybersecurity controls.

Training and Awareness: HIPAA requires covered entities to train their workforce on security awareness and best practices for protecting ePHI. This includes educating employees about cybersecurity threats, such as phishing attacks and malware, and providing guidance on how to securely handle and transmit sensitive data.

Payment Card Industry Data Security Standard (PCI DSS)

Payment Card Industry Data Security Standard, is a set of security standards designed to ensure that companies that process, store, or transmit credit card information maintain a secure environment. Developed by the Payment Card Industry Security Standards Council (PCI SSC), PCI DSS aims to protect cardholder data from theft and fraud. Some key aspects of PCI DSS compliance in cybersecurity includes:

Scope Determination: Organizations must determine the scope of their PCI DSS compliance efforts, identifying all systems, networks, and processes that store, process, or transmit cardholder data. This includes not only the primary systems but also any connected systems and networks that could impact the security of cardholder data.

Security Controls: PCI DSS outlines a set of security controls and best practices that organizations must implement to protect cardholder data. These controls include measures such as encryption, access controls, network segmentation, vulnerability management, and regular security testing.

Compliance Validation: Organizations are required to undergo periodic assessments to validate their compliance with PCI DSS. This may involve self-assessment questionnaires (SAQs) for smaller merchants or on-site assessments conducted by qualified security assessors (QSAs) for larger organizations.

Reporting and Documentation: PCI DSS compliance requires organizations to maintain documentation demonstrating their adherence to the standard. This includes policies, procedures, and records of security testing and remediation activities.

Incident Response: Organizations must have processes and procedures in place to detect, respond to, and report security incidents involving cardholder data. This includes promptly investigating suspected breaches, containing the impact of the incident, and notifying relevant parties as required by law or contractual agreements.

Vendor Management: PCI DSS requires organizations to ensure that third-party service providers who handle cardholder data also maintain adequate security controls. This involves conducting due diligence on vendors, including assessing their compliance with PCI DSS requirements.

Continuous Compliance: PCI DSS compliance is not a one-time event but an ongoing process. Organizations must continuously monitor their security controls, conduct regular security assessments, and address any vulnerabilities or deficiencies to maintain compliance.

Chapter 11: Case study on cloud security breach incidents

Okta (2023):

Breach: Hackers exploited a vulnerability in Okta's customer support system, resulting in the exposure of sensitive customer data of over 134 enterprises. Cause: The service account credential used to access Okta had been saved in the employee's personal Google account. The employee's personal account compromise led to Okta attack.

Remediation: Okta had released features that allow customers to secure their administrative access in a tenant, strengthen session security, and enhance location-based access controls.

GitHub (2021):

Breach: Unauthorized access to GitHub's Git repositories exposed source code of numerous high-profile companies, including Microsoft and Google. Cause: Weak access controls and compromised credentials allowed attackers to access GitHub's internal systems.
Remediation: GitHub enforced multi-factor authentication, improved monitoring capabilities, and conducted a thorough review of access permissions.

Slack (2021):

Breach: A security incident at Slack resulted in unauthorized access to user profile information, including email addresses and hashed passwords.
Cause: Credential stuffing attack leveraging reused passwords from other breaches.
Remediation: Slack forced password resets for affected accounts, implemented stricter authentication mechanisms, and encouraged users to enable two-factor authentication.

T-Mobile (2021):

Breach: Unauthorized access to T-Mobile's systems compromised personal information of over 100 million customers.
Cause: Exploitation of a vulnerability in T-Mobile's network infrastructure.
Remediation: T-Mobile patched the vulnerability, conducted a forensic investigation, and offered affected customers free identity theft protection services.

Colonial Pipeline (2021):

Breach: A ransomware attack on Colonial Pipeline's systems disrupted fuel supply across the East Coast of the United States.

Cause: Lack of robust cybersecurity measures and outdated software left the network vulnerable to exploitation.
Remediation: Colonial Pipeline implemented multi-factor authentication, enhanced network monitoring capabilities, and invested in cybersecurity training for employees.

Microsoft Exchange Server (2021):

Breach: Multiple zero-day vulnerabilities in Microsoft Exchange Server allowed attackers to gain unauthorized access to email accounts of thousands of organizations worldwide.
Cause: Exploitation of unpatched vulnerabilities in Microsoft Exchange Server software.
Remediation: Microsoft released emergency security patches, provided guidance on mitigating the vulnerabilities, and urged organizations to apply the patches immediately.

Twitter (2020):

Breach: Attackers gained access to Twitter's internal systems and compromised accounts of high-profile individuals, including politicians and celebrities, to perpetrate a cryptocurrency scam.
Cause: Social engineering attack targeting Twitter employees to obtain access credentials.
Remediation: Twitter enhanced employee security awareness training, enforced stricter access controls, and improved monitoring of privileged accounts.

SolarWinds (2020):

Breach: Highly sophisticated supply chain attack targeted SolarWinds' Orion software, compromising the networks of numerous government agencies and Fortune 500 companies.
Cause: Compromised software update mechanism allowed attackers to inject malicious code into legitimate software.
Remediation: SolarWinds conducted a comprehensive security audit, enhanced their software development lifecycle processes, and collaborated with law enforcement agencies to investigate the incident.

Capital One (2019):

Breach: A former employee of a cloud service provider gained unauthorized access to Capital One's systems hosted on AWS, resulting in the exposure of sensitive customer data of over 100 million individuals.
Cause: Misconfiguration of a web application firewall allowed the attacker to execute commands to access the data.
Remediation: Capital One immediately fixed the misconfiguration, enhanced their security protocols, and offered identity protection services to affected customers.

Facebook (2019):

Breach: An unprotected database exposed personal information of over 540 million Facebook users, including phone numbers and Facebook IDs.
Cause: Failure to secure the database containing user data.
Remediation: Facebook secured the exposed database, notified affected users, and enhanced their security protocols to prevent similar incidents in the future.

British Airways (2018):

Breach: Magecart attackers inserted malicious code into British Airways' website, intercepting payment information of approximately 380,000 customers.
Cause: Vulnerability in a third-party script used by the website allowed attackers to execute a supply chain attack.
Remediation: British Airways enhanced their website security, conducted a thorough forensic investigation, and offered compensation to affected customers.

Marriott International (2018):

Breach: Hackers gained unauthorized access to Marriott's Starwood guest reservation database, compromising personal information of approximately 500 million guests.

Cause: Long-term undetected access by attackers following the acquisition of Starwood Hotels, exploiting vulnerabilities in their systems.
Remediation: Marriott conducted a comprehensive security audit, implemented advanced threat detection systems, and invested in employee training on cybersecurity best practices.

NASA (2018):

Breach: Unsecured NASA Jet Propulsion Laboratory (JPL) server allowed hackers to steal 500 MB of data, including mission-critical files related to Mars rover projects.
Cause: Lack of multi-factor authentication and weak access controls on the server.
Remediation: NASA improved network segmentation, implemented multi-factor authentication, and conducted extensive cybersecurity training for JPL personnel.

MyFitnessPal (2018):

Breach: Cybercriminals gained unauthorized access to MyFitnessPal's database, compromising personal information of approximately 150 million users.
Cause: Weak security controls allowed attackers to exploit vulnerabilities in MyFitnessPal's systems.
Remediation: MyFitnessPal enforced password resets, enhanced encryption protocols, and provided users with identity protection services.

Equifax (2017):

Breach: Hackers exploited a vulnerability in Apache Struts framework on Equifax's web servers, accessing personal information of 147 million individuals.
Cause: Failure to patch the known vulnerability despite a fix being available.
Remediation: Equifax upgraded their security measures, initiated an internal investigation, and offered free credit monitoring services to affected consumers.

Uber (2016):

Breach: Hackers gained access to Uber's systems, compromising personal information of 57 million users and driver's license information of 600,000 drivers.
Cause: Failure to disclose the breach and pay ransom to the attackers to keep the incident under wraps.
Remediation: Uber implemented a bug bounty program, enhanced encryption protocols, and hired new cybersecurity leadership to oversee remediation efforts.

Slack (2015):

Breach: Slack's user database was compromised, exposing user credentials of approximately 500,000 accounts.
Cause: Unauthorized access to Slack's infrastructure due to weak authentication mechanisms.
Remediation: Slack enforced stronger password policies, implemented multi-factor authentication, and conducted a security audit of their systems.

Home Depot (2014):

Breach: Attackers gained unauthorized access to Home Depot's systems, compromising payment card information of 56 million customers.
Cause: Failure to address vulnerabilities in Home Depot's point-of-sale systems.
Remediation: Home Depot implemented chip-enabled payment terminals, enhanced encryption protocols, and conducted a thorough security audit of their systems.

eBay (2014):

Breach: Hackers gained unauthorized access to eBay's network, compromising personal information of 145 million users.
Cause: Failure to detect unauthorized access to the network for several months.

Remediation: eBay enforced password resets, implemented multi-factor authentication, and improved monitoring capabilities to detect suspicious activities.

JPMorgan Chase (2014):

Breach: Attackers gained unauthorized access to JPMorgan Chase's systems, compromising personal information of 76 million households and 7 million small businesses.
Cause: Weak authentication mechanisms and insufficient network segmentation allowed attackers to infiltrate the network.
Remediation: JPMorgan Chase enhanced network security controls, implemented two-factor authentication, and conducted a comprehensive review of their cybersecurity posture.

Yahoo (2013-2014):

Breach: A series of cyberattacks on Yahoo compromised personal information of over 3 billion user accounts.
Cause: Poor security practices and failure to promptly detect and respond to the breaches.
Remediation: Yahoo implemented stronger encryption protocols, enforced password resets, and invested in cybersecurity talent and technologies.

Adobe Systems (2013):

Breach: Cybercriminals gained access to Adobe's systems, compromising data of 38 million users, including encrypted passwords and credit card information.
Cause: Weak encryption methods employed by Adobe left sensitive data vulnerable to decryption.
Remediation: Adobe enhanced encryption protocols, implemented multi-factor authentication, and notified affected users to change their passwords.

Target Corporation (2013):

Breach: Attackers infiltrated Target's network through a third-party HVAC vendor, compromising payment card data of 40 million customers and personal information of 70 million individuals.
Cause: Lack of segmentation within Target's network allowed the attackers to move laterally and access sensitive systems.
Remediation: Target bolstered network segmentation, enhanced monitoring capabilities, and invested in advanced threat detection technologies.

LinkedIn (2012):

Breach: A hacker gained unauthorized access to LinkedIn's database, compromising passwords of approximately 117 million users.

Cause: Weak encryption methods employed by LinkedIn left passwords susceptible to decryption.
Remediation: LinkedIn enforced password resets for affected users, implemented stronger encryption algorithms, and enhanced security protocols.

Dropbox (2012):

Breach: A Dropbox employee's account was compromised, leading to unauthorized access to a project document containing user email addresses.
Cause: Reuse of passwords across multiple accounts, allowing attackers to access the employee's Dropbox account.
Remediation: Dropbox implemented two-factor authentication, enforced stronger password policies, and enhanced employee security training.

Sony PlayStation Network (2011):

Breach: A cyberattack on Sony's PlayStation Network resulted in the theft of personal information, including credit card details, of approximately 77 million users.
Cause: Inadequate security measures and outdated software left the network vulnerable to exploitation.
Remediation: Sony overhauled their network security infrastructure, enforced stricter access controls, and provided identity theft protection services to affected users.

Table of Contents